PO-WHIMS

by

Jim Morgan

For Joan, as ever

Published by BCF Books
Designed by Ruth Hall
Printed by BookPrintingUK. Bonacia Ltd.
Distribution BCF Books
Contact: cmornement284@gmail.com

Date 2019

ISBN: 978 0 9548512 55

Contents

I proposed to Joan, my wife, on a bench at Charing Cross station. We had just returned from a day's ramble with our rambling club. I warned her that if she married me she would never be rich or even well-to-do. I didn't however tell her that my one ambition in life was to become a poet. Getting what is laughingly called a life was subsidiary to this prime ambition.

Here are the results, a gathering of some sixty years of writing or trying to write poetry. There will be no 'moaning of the bar' (I quote from Tennyson's poem of farewell) when I depart.

It is probably a vain hope that someone somewhere may chance upon these pages and wonder and say to himself or herself, 'Who was he?' Now I even wonder myself.

THE PONGLE WONGLE WOO

The Pongle Wongle Woo

The things that it can do.

It'll weep just like a violin

But bang like a big drum too.

It tinkles it tingles

As coy as a celeste

Then quick as a flash like cymbals clash

Or blare like the brasses best.

On a Friday or a Monday

It's mellow as a cello

But every other Sunday

It's quite a different fellow.

It squeals just like a cornet

Or like an oboe coos

Then varies to a clarinet

With the melancholy blues.

O Pongle Wongle Woo

Whatever will you do?

The others in the orchestra

Are plotting against you

And really who can blame them

Who has a caring soul

For your versatility

Could put them on the dole.

But when the fool conductor

The others tried to shelve

And begged Woo to try to do

The whole of the 1812

Well, hubris is a fate I think

Nothing can forestall -

For Wongle Woo into pieces blew

Itself and the Albert Hall!

A HOLEY END

There's a hole in the sky
It is God's peep-hole
And through it He peers
Down on the puny race of men
Trying to recall
Why He created them
Man & Woman

Several times He regretted
His enormous folly
And tried to expunge
The reckless experiment
But always at the last moment
Relented & gave them another chance

For after all
When they don't enrage
They amuse him
With their furious antics

For all their destructive ways
They harmed nobody but themselves
For when the Universe has had
Enough of their puling and whining
And smashing its things
(That didn't belong to them)
It will swallow them whole

With not even a burp

WITHOUT YOU

Without you
throwing my stick
I'd be a dull
dog indeed

Without you
pulling my strings
I'd be too
laid back

Without you
ringing the changes
I'd be a
dumbbell

Without you
the sun won't rise
I couldn't see
out of my eyes
(to summarize)
upon my honour
I'd be a gonna

THE LITTLE THINGS

the little things of every day

help the poor soul on its way

through the travail of our birth

and our scanted time on earth

as the weaving of the Fates

or our DNA dictates

one poor life much like another

is it worth, Lord all the pother?

the push and pull of greed and fear

the carousel of year on year

the phantom birth of a career?

why all this striving of our dust

for a little itch of lust?

only, it seems, a chosen few

rise to take a higher view

and have a faith to see them through

which makes the spending of our breath

worth the pains of life and death

for the rest, the mortal dross,

blank incomprehension, total loss

when the light fades from their eyes

and the human animal dies

ON WITNESSING A SUDDEN DEATH

The look of death

The same complete exhaustion

The same stillness

The same immediate desertion

Of spirit and soul

From the stalled body

What's left

An object occupying certain space

Old furniture, to be carried away

POEM ON BROWN PAPER

I like you, brown paper!
I like your touch & feel.
You're workmanlike and real.

Your face, tho' plain
And coarse of grain,
I far prefer to any flapper's –
Fancy wrappers.

You endure wind & weather –
Hold together

      Old boots

      Old socks

      Old suits

      Old clocks

And do not easily tear.
I like you, brown paper –
YOU CARE!
GOD GRANT YOU HAIRY STRING!

9

THE BRITISH SERGEANT MAJOR

The British Sergeant Major
Is a model of his kind
Brave, resourceful, generous,
And rather broad behind.

Political correctness
Is not his greatest suit
He treats us all impartially
Damns every new recruit

We're all 'a ruddy shower'
And 'whatever did 'e do
To 'ave us wished upon 'im
Such a dozy looking crew'

'Is language, well, I'd tell you
But I see there's ladies 'ere,
Enough to make a bargee blush
And blubber in 'is beer.

We often 'ear 'im comment
How strange 'e always gets

The scraping of the barrel
Or ruddy teachers' pets.

The hofficers adore 'im
And on 'im they depend
For they know the men obey 'im
And be with 'im at the end

And when we advance in line
Our bayonets at the ready
His is the voice will quietly say
'Steady boys now, steady!'

MEMORY OF WALES

Yellow gorse flaming on the mountain side
The spring-heeled lambs bouncing on the rocks
Everywhere the music of running waters
Rinsing the ears like singing bells

This is Wales, land of my fathers,
Here still persists the ancient tongue
In the mouths of the children
Playing in the school playground
On the dry lips of the old men and women
Gossiping on corners

The chapels where once they worshipped
Once raised their mighty halleluiahs
To their God, are derelict now
And in their place plethoric supermarkets
What sounds now is not the preacher's hwyl
Or a full voiced choir moving the heavens to tears
But the inane chatter of TV hucksters
The mindless staccato beat of 'pop'

Where shall we look for a new song

Where to turn to escape the brutal

Obliquity of our man-made hells?

The priest poet Hopkins cried in faith

'There lives the dearest freshness deep down things'

Oh Lord be with us when we doubt this

Forgive us when we fear it is not so

Open our hearts, our eyes, our ears

So we may hear again these voices

Assaulting heaven with their triumphant song

MY LEFTY DAYS ARE OVER

My lefty days are over
We are all Tories now
Nosda, Aneurin Bevan
And all his Welsh powwow

I have a little nest egg
A place in a nice town
Money doesn't worry me
And bills don't get me down

But I confess there's something
Missing in my life
I can't quite put my finger on
It cannot be the wife

One day now is like another
On radio or TV
The world conspires to smother
The cry for liberty

With round the clock surveillance

In which we all collude

Prying in every corner

Of our precious solitude

Big Brother or Big Sister

Transgendered tyrannize

Swopping one with another

Before our very eyes

So what's the vital difference

To whom shall I complain?

When everyone's together now

Wired to one collective brain

INVOCATION

Roll on, thou lubberly world, roll on!

Like an old tyre as kids we beat along
With a bit of stick
Obediently rolling down slopes
Impossibly up steep inclines
Staggering crazily here & there
Groggy under our pummelling
Until at last
It fell over on its side
In the dust of the gutter
With a flat sigh
And lay still

DRUNK

He kept hitting the pavement hard
But not as hard as the pavement hit him.
Between rounds he staggered around
Looking for his corner, abruptly sitting down
On a stool that wasn't there. He was game
I'll say that for him, but he was counted out
At last, flat on his back, seeing stars.

MOBILE

Talking away, yapping away
Mobiles plugged in their ears
Whatever do they talk about
The dreary little dears?

In the cold meat section
'Is there anything you want?'
While mum's a minute's walk away
Buying a potted plant.

Walking away, talking away
Oblivious to all beside
Her closest chum's cherished secrets
Loudly publicize?

And pity the poor commuters
Trapped on a crowded train
Who have to hear her inane rap
Adding to the strain.

How is it that this nation
A few short years before
Famous for its reticence
Now can't stop its jaw, jaw, jaw?

WORLD WIDE WEB

"Won't you walk into my parlour?" said the spider to the fly,

"We'll communicate quite nicely and soon see eye to eye.

Forgive my clumsy fumblings we're all new to this game,

'Democratic globalism' Don't you think's a catchy name?

Look at all your fellow creatures, how harmoniously they

hum,

As one by one they tumble into my capacious tum,

There will always be reactionaries opposed to any change,

But as our web grows wider none will be beyond our range.

There is not the smallest cranny now can escape the web

Enlightenment will filter down to the very lowest pleb

All will see and act together as in a cosmic trance

'SO, WILL YOU, WON'T YOU, WILL YOU, WON'T YOU,

COME AND JOIN THE DANCE?' "

EGO

My father always warned me
Not to stare too long at the mirror
Or the devil will jump out of my eyes.
So I still avert my gaze
Not wishing to catch the devil
Though sometimes for devilment
I look long at that sad face
Facing me, the sullen mouth
Those disappointed eyes,
The lines graved on each cheek.
No devil affronts me, only time
Doing its dirty work.

SONG

The fishes that dart through the ocean
The birds that delight in the air,
The clear running river, the flowering
                                    meadow,
God gave into our care.

But we poison the fish in the ocean
And we slaughter the birds of the air,
A clear running river we turn to a sewer
And flowering meadows are rare.

We spit on the glory of being
And darken the stars in the sky;
The cleverness devil delivers to evil
Our children who sicken and die.

O give us the grace to be simple,
To heed the small voices within
To reverence nature and every creature
Love as our innocent kin.

FRED

Fred

lived in a shed

it was not a big shed

but it had a bed

whereon to lay his head

and a roof, a table and a door

it was enough for Fred

who was used to being poor

but people said

'it should not be permitted

he is insanitary and old

and probably half-witted

if truth were told'

and so this led

sundry officials

to visit Fred

and having read

'relevant sections of the appropriate act'

they pulled down the shed

and had him removed

to a very nice old people's home

in Frome

where he did not live happily ever after

but was soon dead

'There's gratitude' they said

Poor Fred.

MISSING LINK

Learn to live within your skin
Learn to love the skin you're in
Be it fat or be it thin.
And if sometimes it doesn't fit
And you long to be out of it
Well, maybe you are growing wings –
I have heard of stranger things.
Think of Darwin's odd surmises,
Life is full of such surprises.
For new species to appear
Someone must be pioneer.
So when you itch and fidget – think
You may be the MISSING LINK!

CATS SLEEP AND POETRY

A daffodil sun
gladdens the morning
polishing the furniture
lighting up the wall

I put down my book
luxuriating in its warmth
its brightness
and close my eyes
trying to retrieve
from oblivion
last night's dream

it was of cats

I can still feel
the electric brush of their fur
hear their throaty purr

their paws pad of needles

their rough tongues

sandpapering my hand

and I think

how beautiful the world is

and I think

gratefully of the dead

who have so enhanced my life

and wonder where they are now

and if there are in heaven

such creatures as sun and cats

and sleep and poetry

ORIGIN OF THE SPECIES

Charlie Darwin

Aint my darlin'

His 'Origin of Species' is not for me

I descend from Adam

And his unruly madam

Not from a monkey dropped out of a tree

RANDOM THOUGHTS

1. (Apologies to R.L. Stevenson)

   'The world is so full of a number of things'

   I'm sure we should all be happy as kings

   Why then have things not got better but worser?

   Things rule us now & not vice- versa

2. The Queen Mum

   Even in a media scrum

   Still beams, benign

   Casting her pearls before swine

3. *Remembrance Sunday*

   Yes, remember those who died

   And yearly wear a poppy with pride

   But in the silence remember with shame

   The things we asked them to do in our name

4. *After Longfellow*

   Lives of great men all remind us

   How much happier we should be

Had their doting mothers drowned them

In their bawling infancy

5. *R.I.P.*

It edges nearer every day

No matter what you do or say

Few will worry, few will grieve

And this is all I have to leave.

Once I thought I had the call

But nothing came of it at all:

Just scribbles on a prison wall

6. *Advice to a Young Husband*

If you want a quiet life

Never argue with your wife

Yes – it's true you are much bigger

But she's so much faster on the trigger

MORE RANDOM THOUGHTS

1. The muse is never 'a bit on the side'
   If she takes you it is for life as a bride
   Though the marriage be stormy
   And you quarrel and curse
   You're stuck with her now
   For better or verse

2. She was one of those strenuous girls
   Living with her was a battle
   Like being one of a football crowd
   And you by the guy with the rattle

3. Whatever fate decrees
   I endeavour to be ready
   Humbly down on my knees
   Clutching my old teddy

4. *Transgendering*

I may be a he or a she

It hardly matters to me

In shirt or a dress

I am more or less -

The creature God meant me to be

5. *On a Certain Racial Slur*

Dafydd had a little lamb

They say he shagged her nightly

And when she cried 'Mama, Mama'

He said 'Yes, I think I knew her slightly'

AS HOUSMAN MIGHT SAY

Youth's bulging dreams

Part at the seams

The gold dust spills away

A flaccid sack

That sighs, alack

Is left and all's to pay

A HANDFUL OF HAIKUS

1. Old man in his chair
       Nodding over his paper
       Breathes a long last sigh

2. Uttering prayers
       Like striking dodgy matches
       In the windy dark

3. The days, the weeks, the years
       Tediously turn their wheels
       Slow train to nowhere

4. Delighting the eye
       Green and yellow daffodils
       Jubilant with spring

5.   Late sun through a tear

    In a cloud's pocket spilling

    Silver on the sea

6.   Trees have things to say

    If only you will listen

    And open your ears

7.   Staring, a blank screen

    Which is another nothing

    Posing as something

8.   In the winter's grey

    A robin's tiny bonfire

    Warming our cold